# Maggie the Magical Unicorn
## Coloring Book

By:

Sarah C Hayes

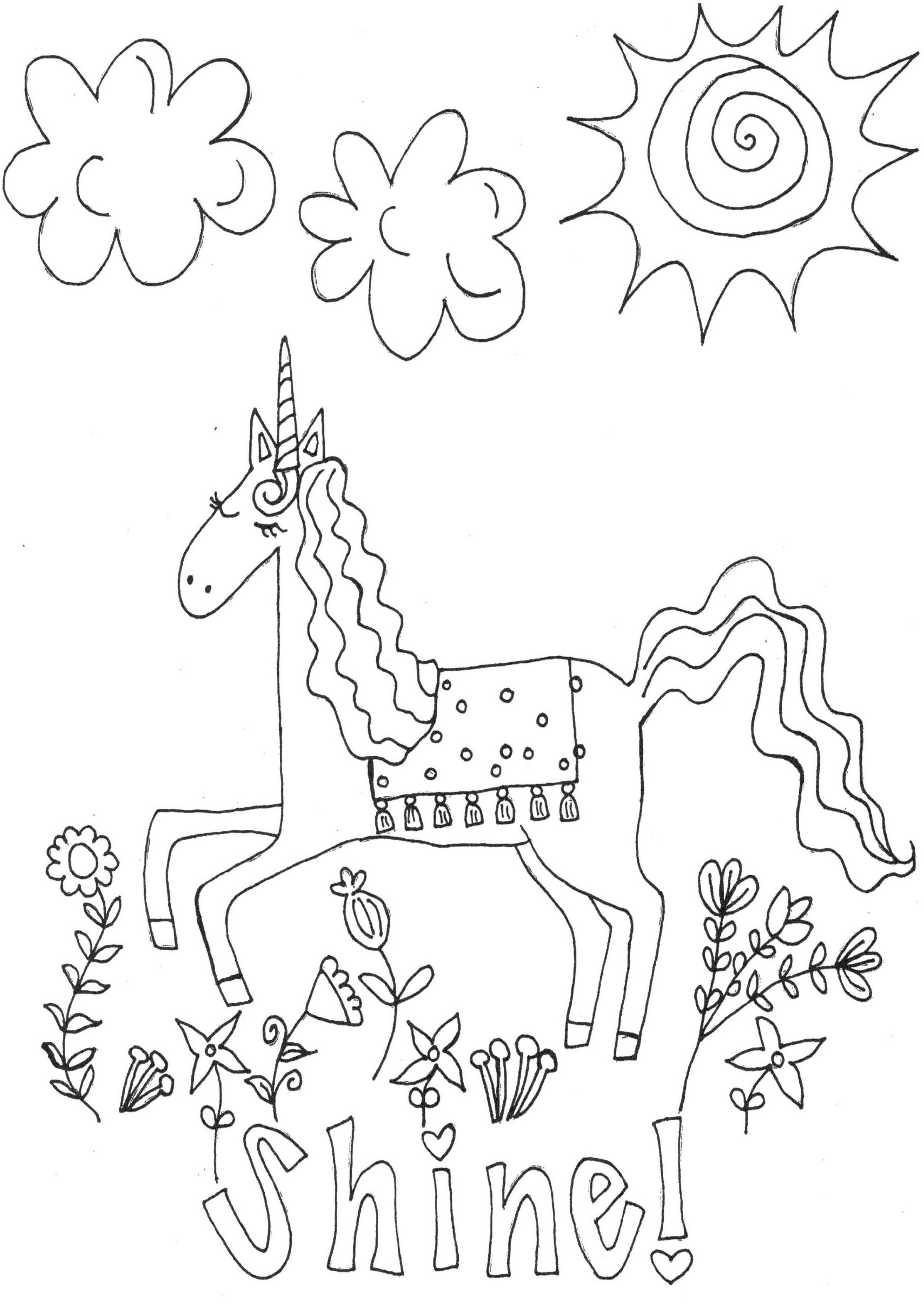
Shine!

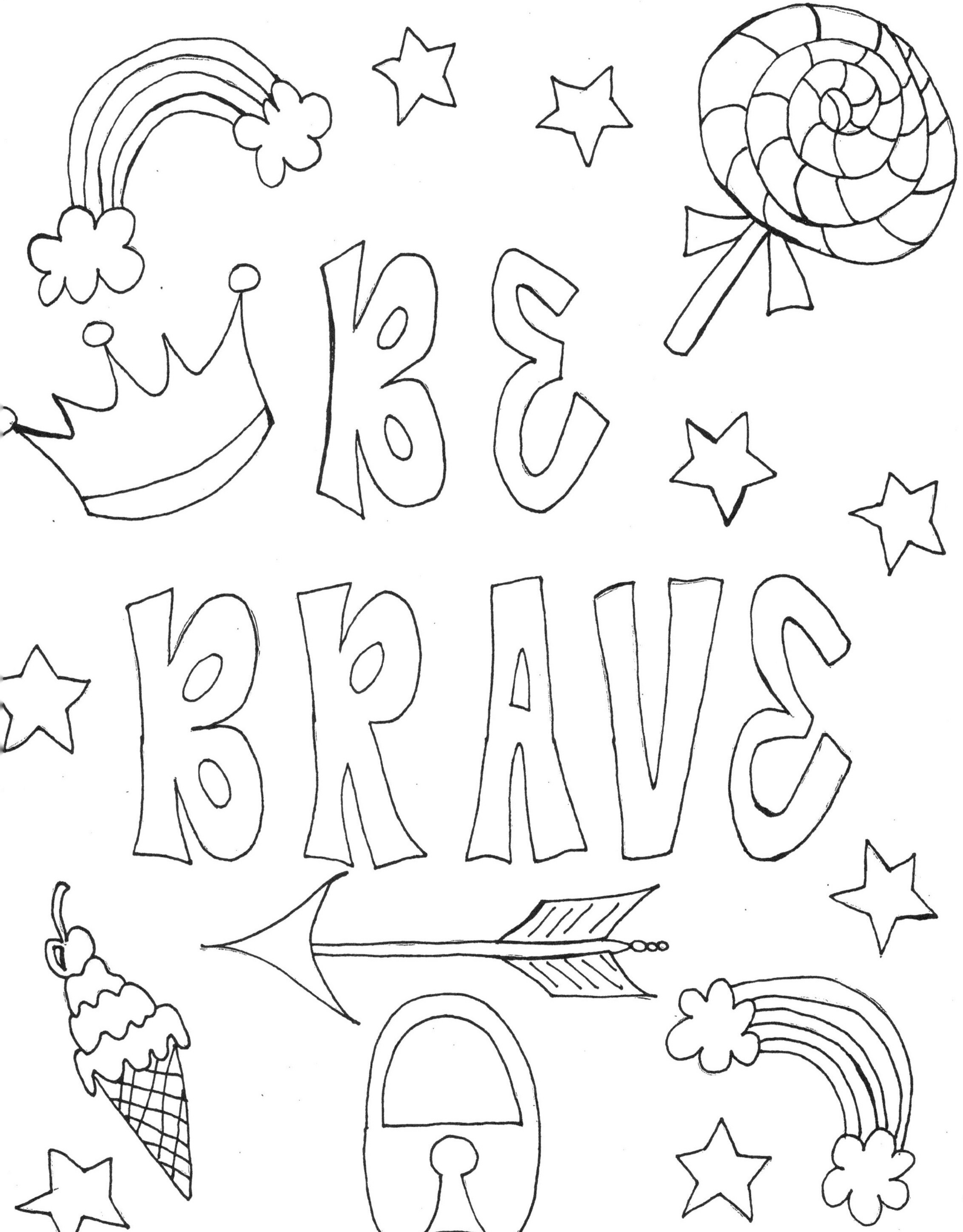
BE
BRAVE

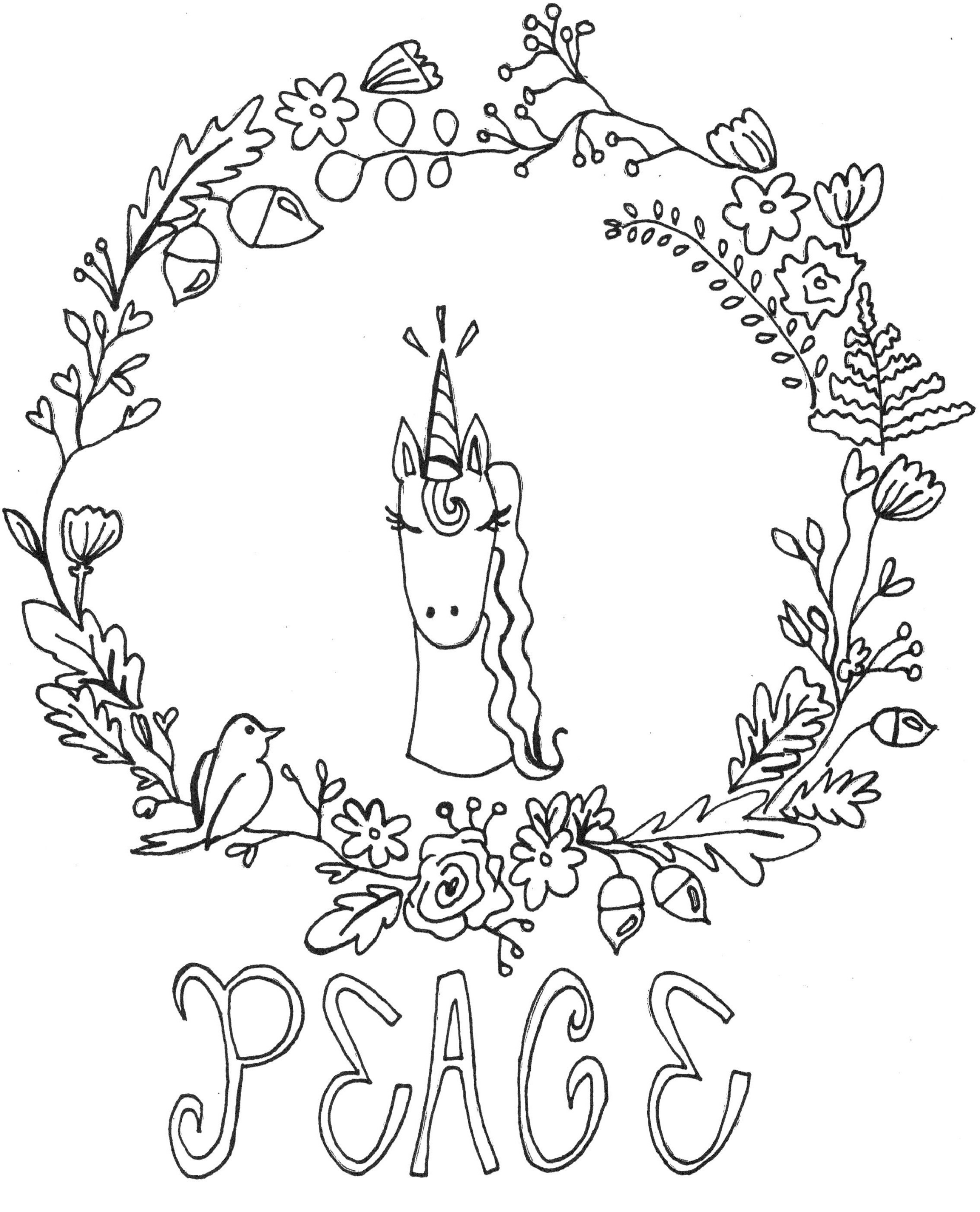
PEACE

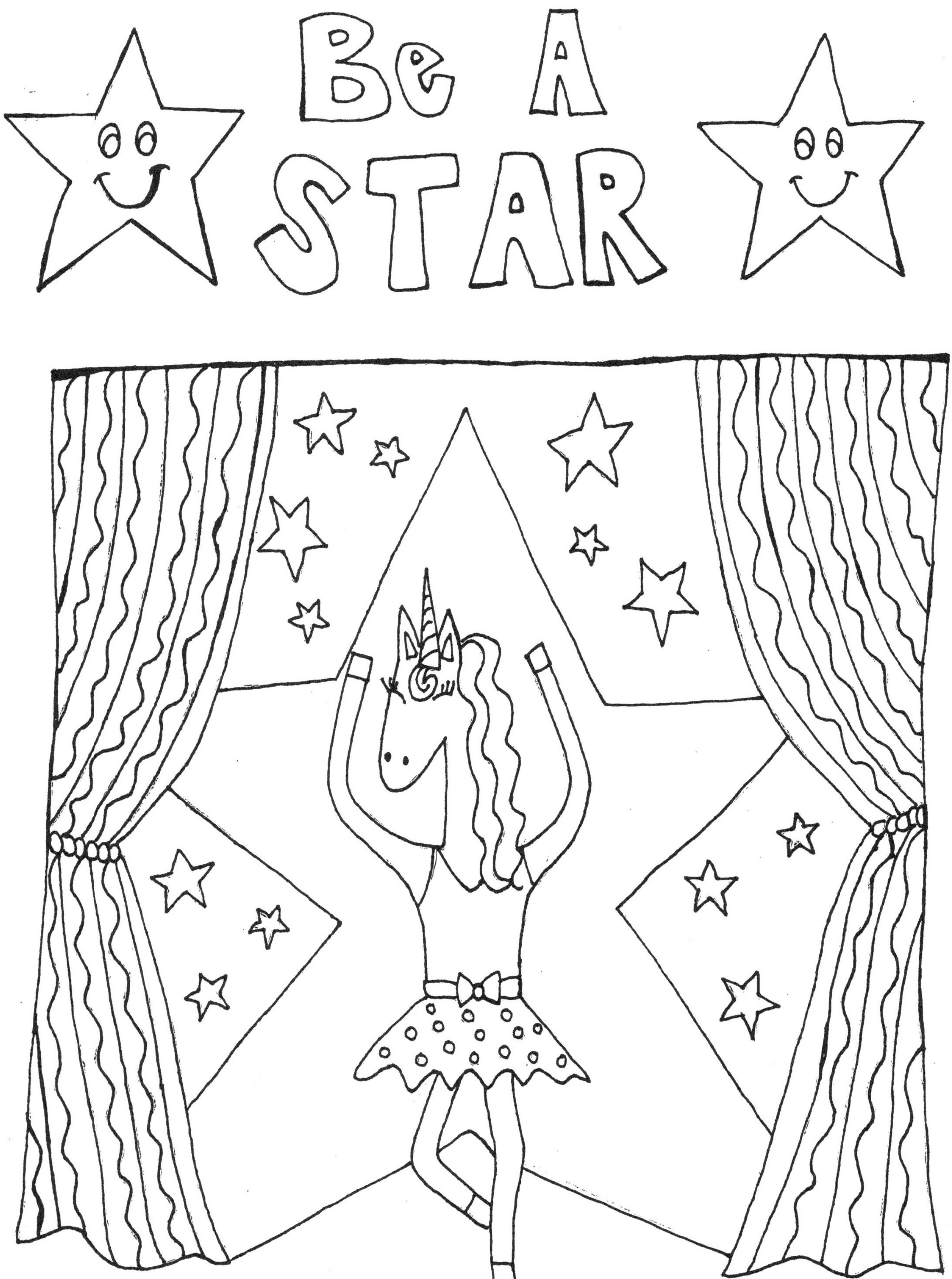
Be A
STAR

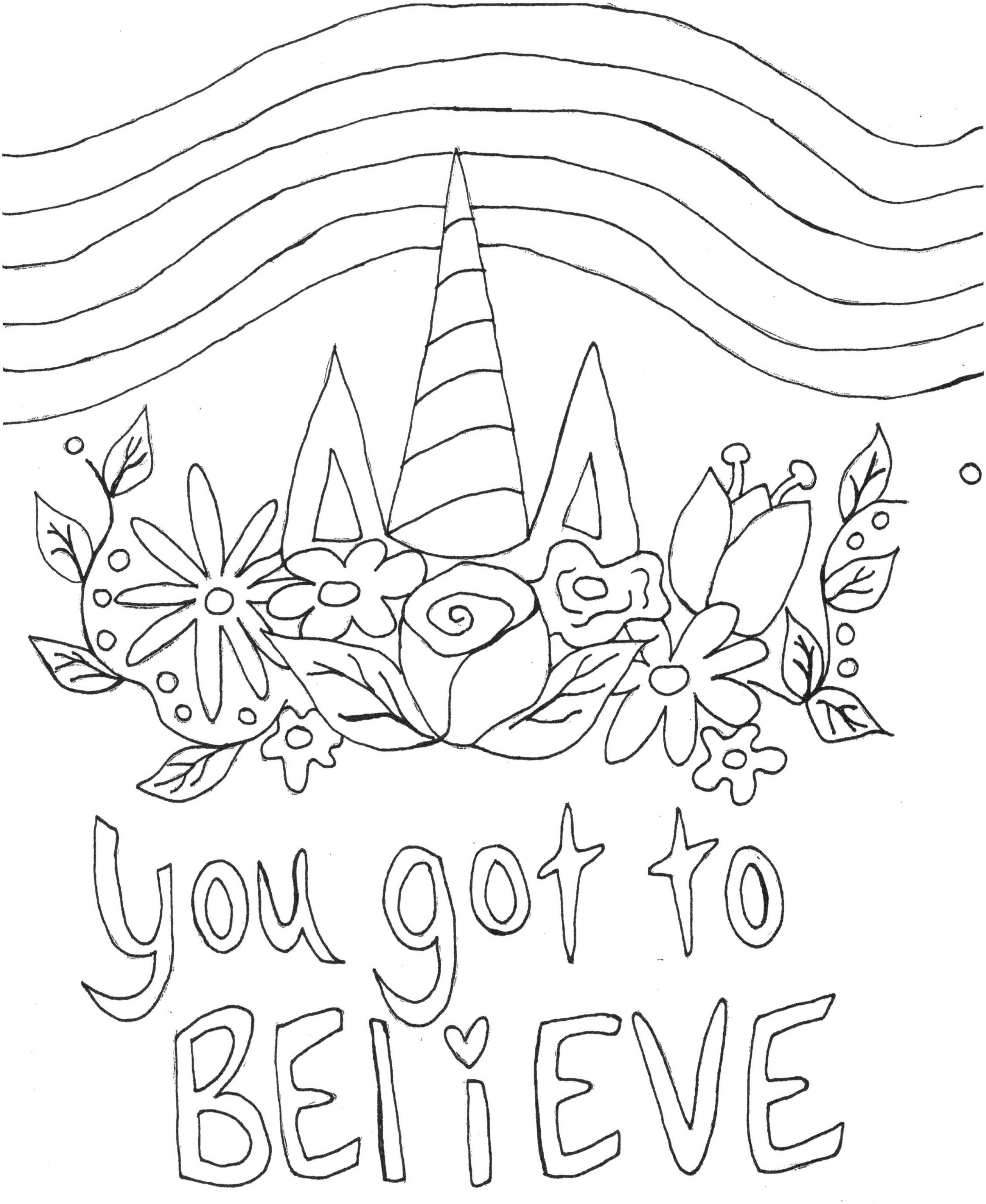
You got to
BELiEVE

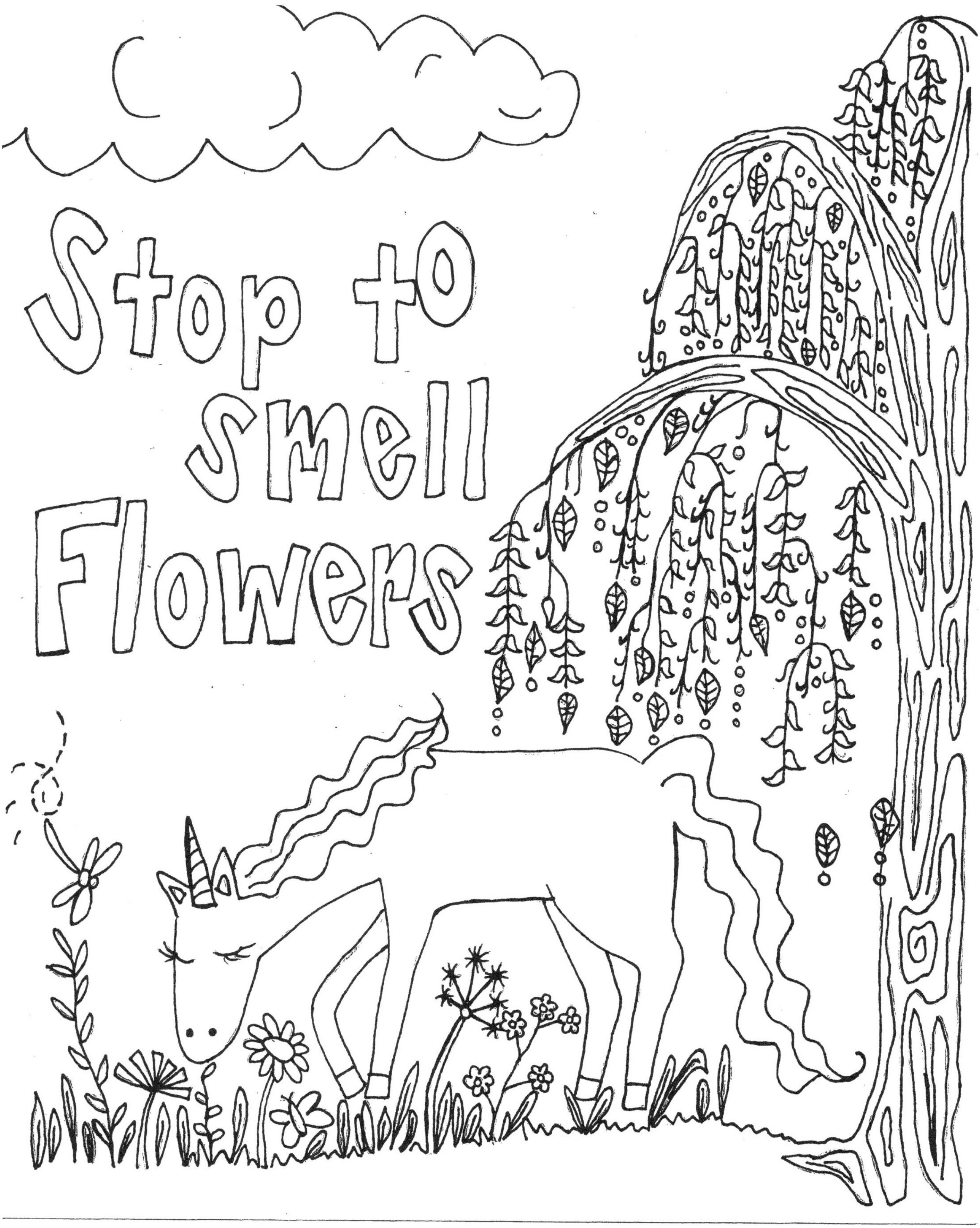
Stop to
smell
Flowers

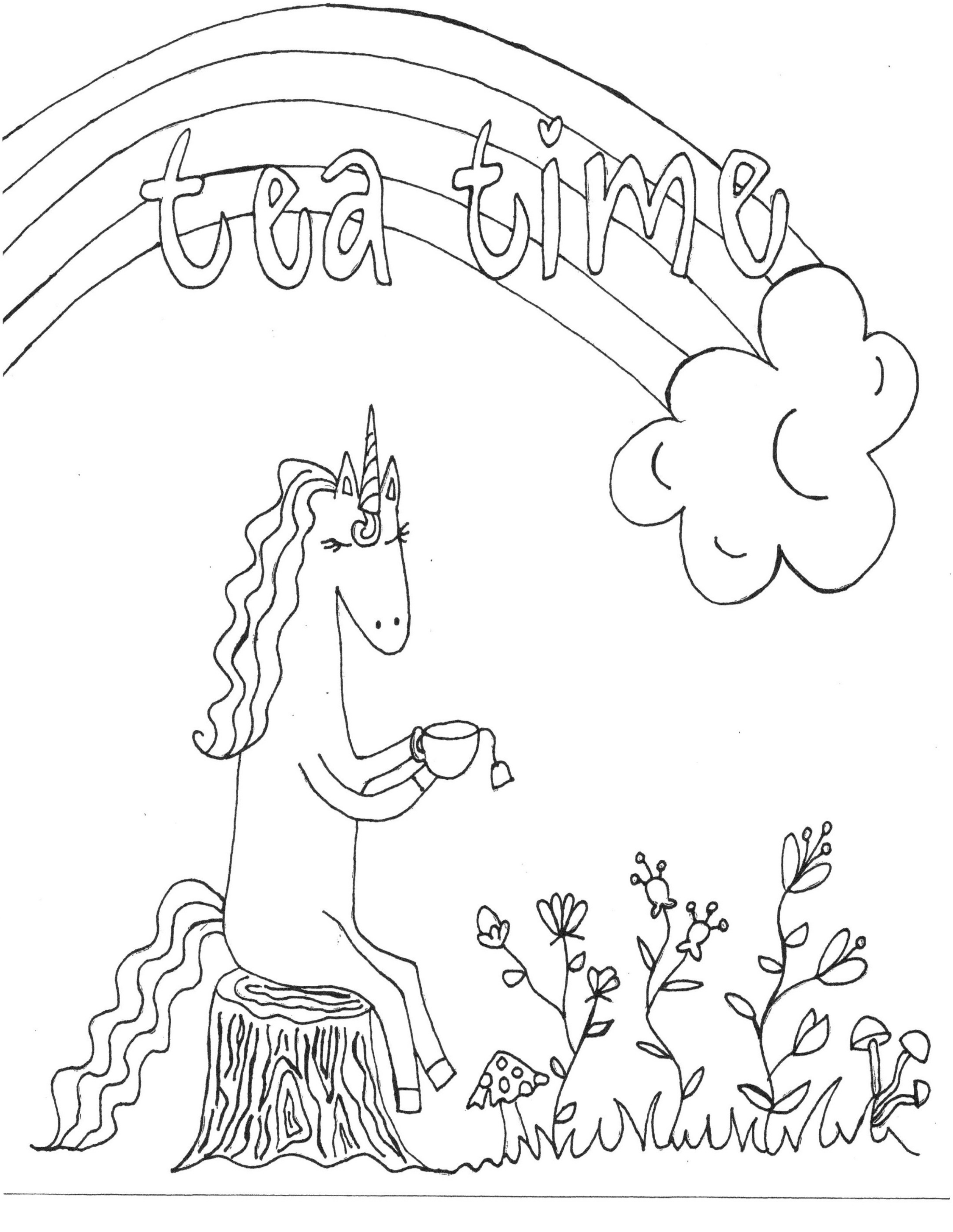
tea time

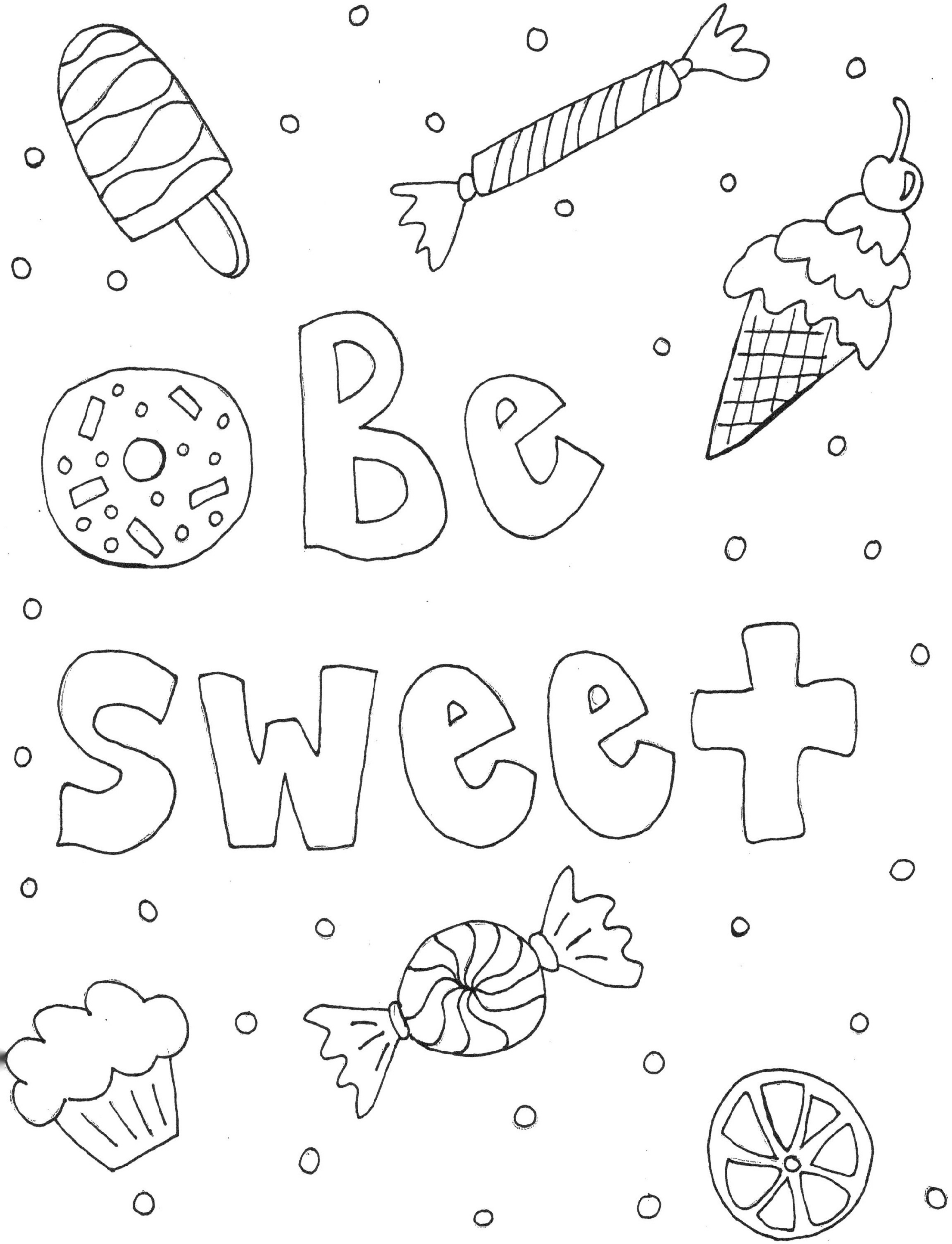
Be
Sweet

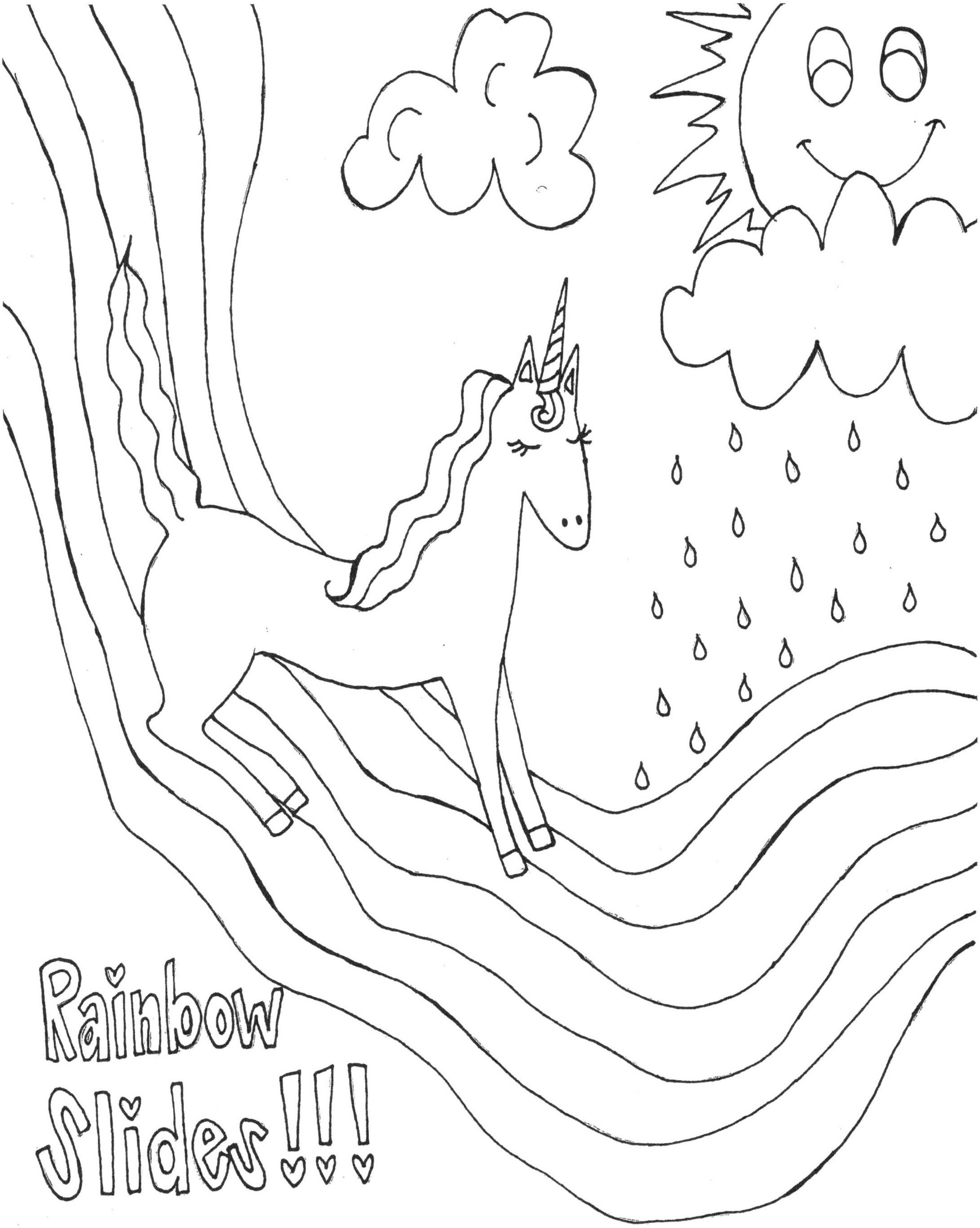
Rainbow
Slides!!!

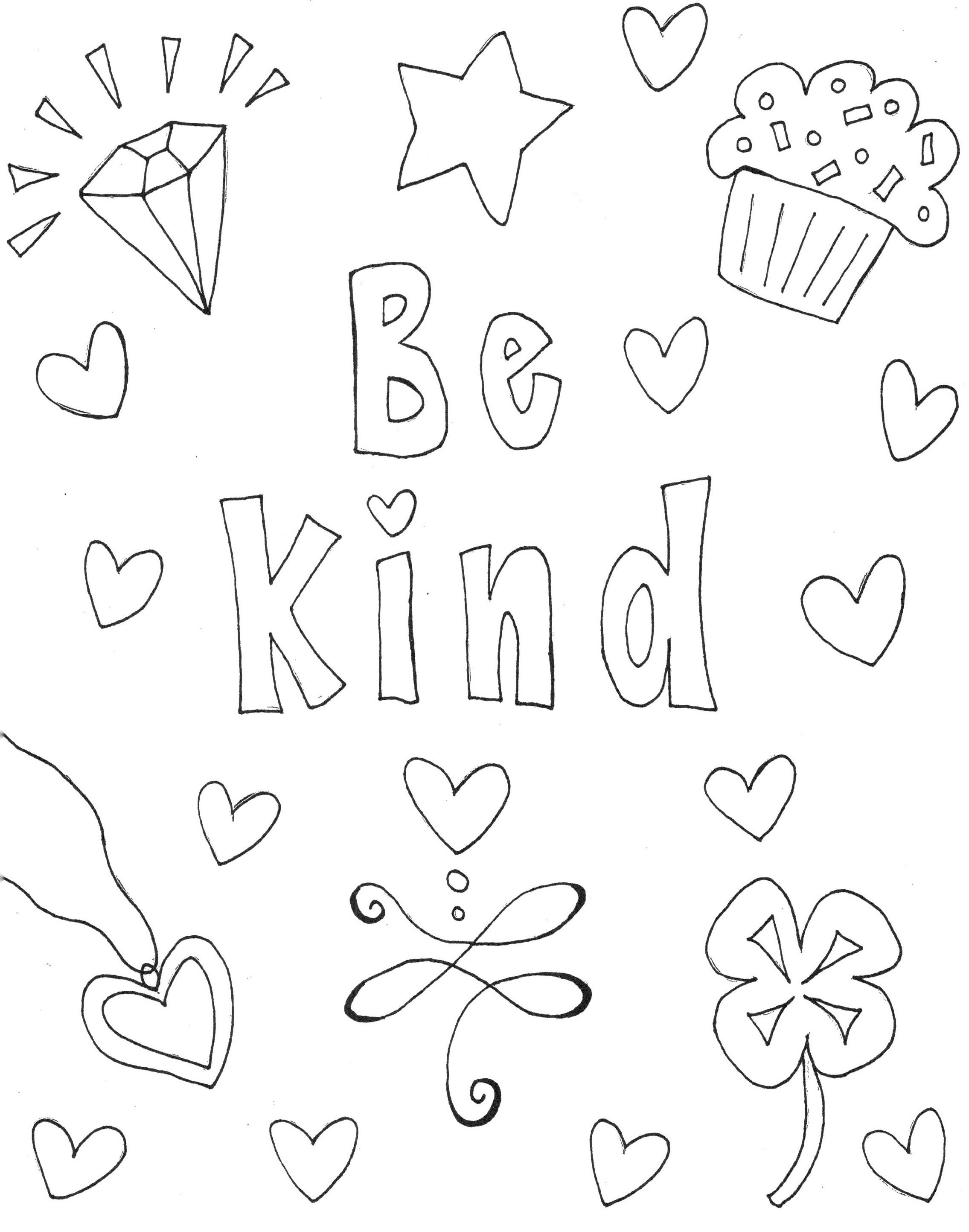
Be
Kind

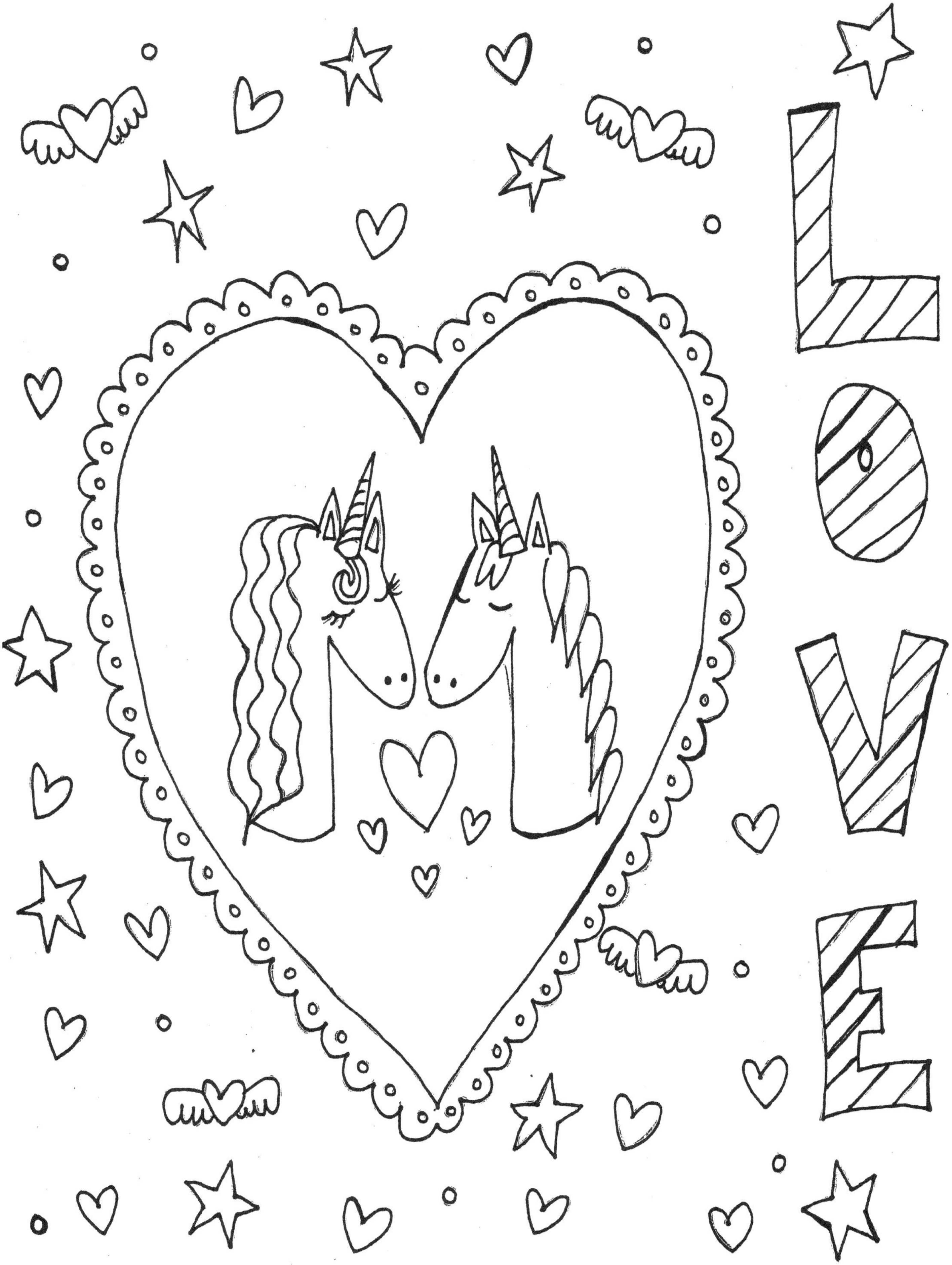
LOVE

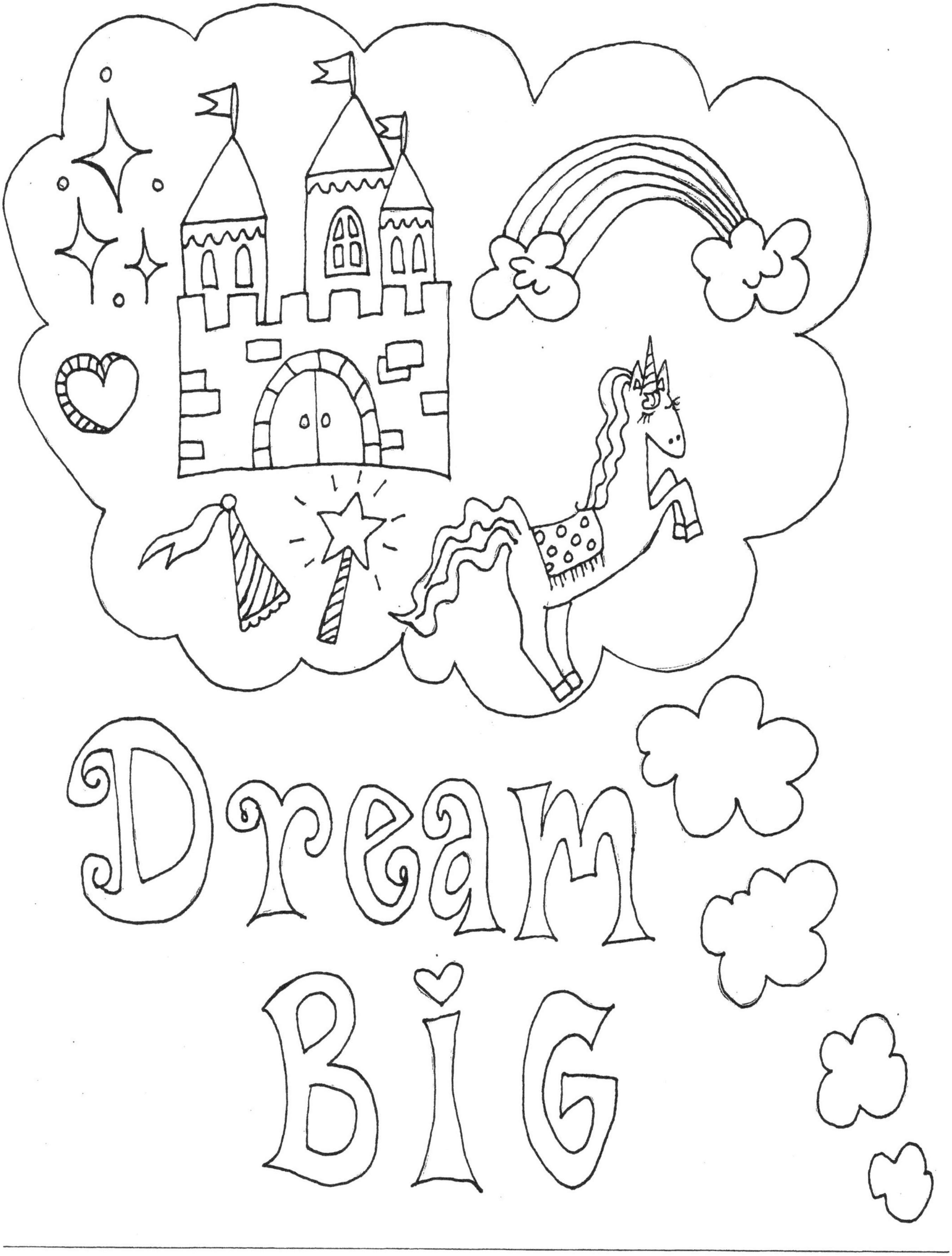
Dream
Big

www.ingramcontent.com/pod-product-compliance
Lightning Source LLC
Chambersburg PA
CBHW081653220526
45468CB00009B/2628